Rugby Run

Tom and Kim were watching rugby.

"Do you like rugby?" said Kim.

"Yes, I do like rugby," said Tom.

SAVING THE DAY

Contents

Stories
illustrated by
Steve May
and
Tom Percival

Heinemann

In this story

 Tom

 Kim

 A robber

 A policeman

Tricky words

- watching
- rugby
- fast
- lady's
- robber
- policeman

Introduce these tricky words and help the reader when they come across them later!

Story starter

Tom and Kim were watching rugby in the park. Tom liked rugby but he didn't think he could run fast enough to play rugby. Then a robber took a lady's bag.

"Rugby is cool," said Tom.
"But I am no good at rugby.
I can't run fast."

"Look, Tom!" said Kim.
"Look at that man!
He has got that lady's bag.
He is a robber!"

"I can stop him," said Tom.

"No, Tom," said Kim.
"The man is too big.
You can't stop him."

Tom ran at the robber.

The robber ran fast,
but Tom ran faster.

Tom got the robber.
"Got you!" he said.

"Aaargh!" said the robber.

A policeman saw Tom.

"Good job, Tom!"
said the policeman.
"I saw you stop the robber."

"Good job, Tom," said Kim.
"You got the robber.
You can run fast."

"Yes," said Tom. "I can run fast. I *am* good at rugby!"

Quiz

Text Detective

- What did the robber steal from the lady?
- Why did Tom say he was good at rugby?
- Do you think Tom was brave?

Word Detective

- **Phonic Assessment:** Blending three phonemes

  Page 8: Sound out the three phonemes (sounds) in 'ran'. Can you blend them?
- Page 9: Sound out the three phonemes (sounds) in 'got'. Can you blend them?
- Page 10: Sound out the three phonemes (sounds) in 'job'. Can you blend them?

Super Speller

Can you spell these words from memory?

you   stop   saw

HA! HA! HA!

Q What do you call two robbers?

A A pair of nickers.

Before Reading

In this story

 Sir Bold

 Hal

 Sir Crusher

Tricky words

- dungeon
- tried
- locked
- heard
- trick
- noise
- behind
- cheered

Introduce these tricky words and help the reader when they come across them later!

Story starter

Sir Bold was a poor knight who lived long ago. He had a faithful servant called Hal and an old horse called Flash. One day, Sir Bold's enemy, Sir Crusher, threw Sir Bold into his dungeon.

Escape!

Sir Bold was fed up.
He was in the dungeon.

He tried the door.
But it was locked.

"I wish Hal was here,"
said Sir Bold.
"He would get me out."

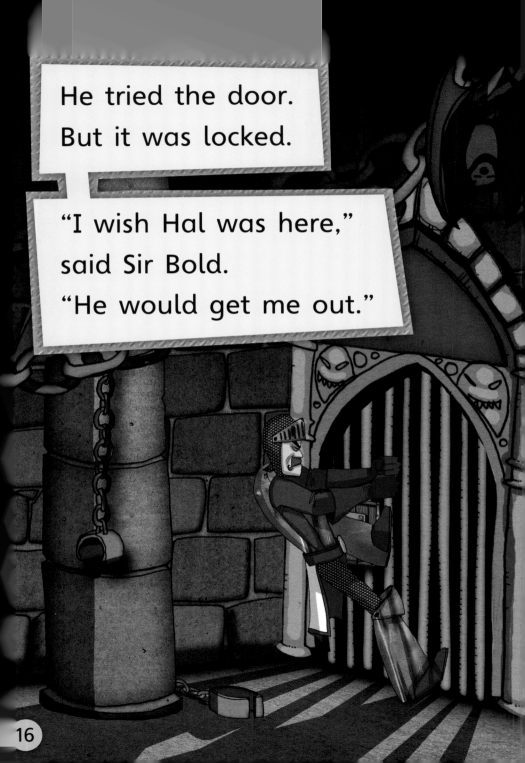

He tried the window.
But it was locked.

"I wish Hal was here,"
said Sir Bold.

"Get me out!" said Sir Bold.

Hal heard Sir Bold.

"Where are you?" said Hal.

"In the dungeon," said Sir Bold.

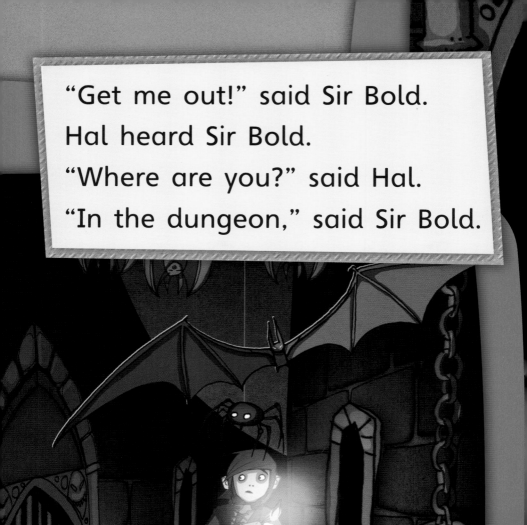

"I will get you out," said Hal.
"You must trick Sir Crusher.
Make a noise, then Sir Crusher
will think you are getting out."

"I will," said Sir Bold.
He ran at the door.

BANG!

Sir Crusher heard the noise.
He ran into the dungeon.
Sir Bold hid behind the door.

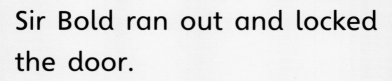

Sir Bold ran out and locked the door.
Sir Crusher was cross.
He could not get out.

Hal and Sir Bold cheered
and cheered.
"You have tricked Sir Crusher,"
said Hal.
"Now Sir Crusher is fed up!"

Quiz

Text Detective

- Who helped Sir Bold to escape?
- Who is the cleverer – Hal or Sir Bold? Why?
- What do you think Sir Crusher will do next?

Word Detective

- **Phonic Assessment:** Blending three phonemes
  Page 15: Sound out the three phonemes
  (sounds) in 'fed'. Can you blend them?
- Page 17: Sound out the three phonemes
  (sounds) in 'wish'. Can you blend them?
- Page 21: Sound out the three phonemes
  (sounds) in 'ran'? Can you blend them?

Super Speller

Can you spell these words from memory?

here   said   into

HA! HA! HA!

Q What does Sir Crusher's mum do
before he goes to sleep?

A She kisses him good-knight.